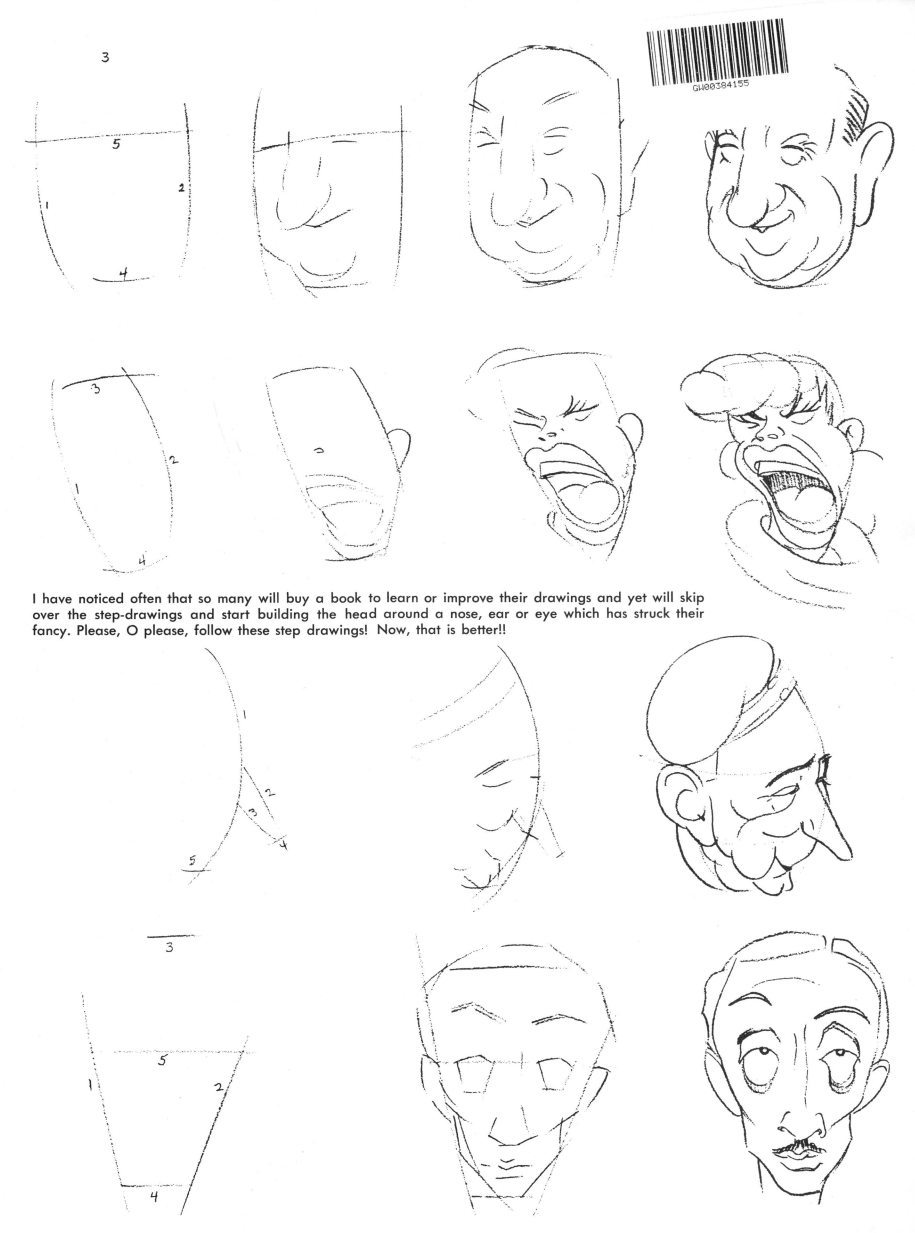

I have noticed often that so many will buy a book to learn or improve their drawings and yet will skip over the step-drawings and start building the head around a nose, ear or eye which has struck their fancy. Please, O please, follow these step drawings! Now, that is better!!

1

now, ink in

NO. 3

The CARTOONIST WORKS AS HARD ON CHARACTER STUDIES AS AN ARTIST DOES ON A PORTRAIT, SO DO NOT BE DISCOURAGED OR EXPECT TOO MUCH OF YOURSELF AT FIRST. IT WILL COME WITH LOTS OF PRACTICE.

*T*HIS IS YOUR FIRST AND MOST IMPORTANT STEP IN LAYING OUT YOUR DRAWINGS FOR SALE, AND MUST NOT BE SKIPPED, IT IS SIMPLE, SO DO NOT MAKE A HARD JOB OF IT.

LINE 5

STEP 2

*T*HIS SPACE WE CHOOSE FOR OUR DRAWING, WHICH WE CAN MAKE ANY SIZE SO LONG AS WE SQUARE LINE 5 WITH LINE 1 AND WHERE-EVER LINE 5 CROSSES DIAGONAL LINE, THAT IS OUR MEASUREMENT FOR LINE 6.

*I*F YOU WILL FOLLOW THIS SIMPLE WAY OF LAYING OUT YOUR DRAW-ING, YOU CAN MAKE IT ANY SIZE AND IT WILL ALWAYS REDUCE TO THE SIZE 1, 2, 3, 4. NOW BLOCK IN YOUR DRAW-ING, AS ON NEXT PAGE.

DIAGONAL LINE

LINE 6

LINE 3

STEP 1

B

LINE 1

LINE 4

6"

A

LINE 2

4⅜"

STEP 1

MAKE LINE 1 AND 2 WHICH MUST BE AT RIGHT AN-GLES, SO HOLD TRIANGLE SOLID SO IT WILL NOT SLIP. YOU CAN USE T SQUARE AND ANGLE IF EASIER FOR YOU. MEASURE UP ON LINE 1 SIX INCHES AND ACROSS ON LINE 2, 4⅜ INCHES. THIS IS THE SPACE YOUR DRAW-ING WILL FILL IN MAGAZINE. USE T SQUARE TO DRAW LINE 3 AND 6 AND ANGLE TO DRAW LINE 4. (CHECK WITH RULER TO SEE THAT LINES 1 AND 4 AND LINES 2 AND 3 ARE THE SAME LENGTH.) DRAW DIAGONAL LINE THROUGH A AND B. THIS IS ALL THE MEAS-UREMENTS YOU NEED. NOW THAT WASN'T HARD WAS IT?

The

PENCIL BLOCKING-IN YOU MAKE SHOULD LOOK SOMETHING LIKE THIS. IT CAN BE MADE ON THIN PAPER AND TRANSFERRED TO YOUR BRISTOL-BOARD WITH GRAPHITE TRACING PAPER — (BUY AT YOUR ART STORE). DO NOT USE TYPEWRITER CARBON. DRAW DIRECTLY ON BRISTOL BOARD WITH LIGHT BLUE OR BLACK PENCIL IF YOU CHOOSE. THE FIRST WAY WILL KEEP YOUR DRAWING CLEANER. CLEAN YOUR DRAWING WITH ART GUM BUT BE CAREFUL NOT TO GRAY YOUR INK LINES.

I F YOU INTEND MAKING COMICS YOUR PROFESSION, START SAVING GOOD JOKES. THERE IS A FINE FIELD FOR SPOT OR SINGLE-FRAME DRAWINGS. YOUR WORK MUST BE CLEAN-CUT, RIGHT SIZE, EASY TO REPRODUCE AND IF YOU WILL FOLLOW THESE FOUR PAGES AS A PATTERN, YOU CANNOT GO FAR WRONG.

DRAWING STRAIGHT LINES WITH BRUSH

DRAWING STRAIGHT LINE WITH RULING PEN

RULER

NO. 1 BRUSH

NO. 3 BRUSH

$\mathcal{Y}$OUR ORIGINAL DRAWING WILL LOOK LIKE THIS. WHEN REDUCED AND YOU SEE IT IN THE MAGAZINE IT WILL LOOK LIKE THE SMALL ONE ON OPPOSITE PAGE. TAKE YOUR MEASUREMENT FROM THE NEWSPAPER OR MAGAZINE TO WHICH YOU ARE GOING TO SUBMIT YOUR DRAWING.

*A*lex' blocking-in is simple, direct and tells the story even in the first sketch. All artists develop a pet way of arriving at their finished drawing and you will do the same.

*M*any artists make their sketch on tracing paper or thin paper which they can fuss with, then trace it on to a clean sheet of Bristol board; in this way you can have a clean start. Do NOT use a typewriter carbon sheet. You can buy the pencil tracing paper at your art store or use a soft pencil and make your own. Use a hard pointed lead pencil, (4-H or 6-H) for transferring on to your clean paper.

The pencil blocking-in should have just enough drawing to give you your guide lines, then you can do the solid blacks and details with your brush, (pen, if you prefer).

Go to a sketch class, draw from still life, live models, etc. You can never get enough drawing—every one you do will make your work that much better.

This "Near-Sighted Lover" idea I sold years ago. To get Alex' conception of the same idea I asked him to make a drawing, with his way of developing it and blocking-in. Now, you try your hand at it, using any sort of fowl, animal or bird. If I had it to do over, I think it would be a very cock-sure bird with chest out, derby hat and all the trimmings, large glasses, yes, making love to the clothespin. People get a bigger laugh out of the discomfiture of the stuck-up, always-right, big guy, than they do out of the under-dog, little fellow; we sort of pity him. Always work for a contrast in ideas, yet keep your drawing simple.

"THE NEAR SIGHTED LOVER"

You will find Alex' letter very interesting and his example an excellent way to start your profession. Art Schools are fine, but there is nothing that can take the place of good old experience in an Art Department or around artists who are making a living at the work.

Study all the original drawings you can and meet artists who are doing the work you are interested in. Most of them are glad to give you a lift but remember, their time is valuable, so do not take up much of it.

"THE NEAR SIGHTED LOVER"

9

1

2

3

Dear Mr. Foster:-

Here are the contributions from me. It makes me real proud to be picked by you as one of your contributors. If I have achieved any measure of success in the cartoon field, I owe it all to my morgue, (clipping file of drawings) of which I make extensive use. Cartooning to me does not come easy, as some people may think. It is real work, particularly since I have never had any formal art training. I firmly believe that if I had taken some time to attend art school and learn the fundamentals of art, my work would probably show it immediately.

I got my cartoon schooling right on the Times, watching the now famous cartoonists, Bod Day, Ted Gale, Bruce Russell, Cliff McBride, Jimmy Hatlc., etc at work. I am also a great admirer of Russell Patterson and Roy Nelson.

Have been working on the Times for nearly 19 years. Started as an office boy and graduated to the Art Dept., not as cartoonist but as photo retoucher and layout man, in fact I still lend a hand at it.

As to my work, I believe I have evolved a style of cartoon that is effective for newspapers. I use brush #1 for all work. I try to make black and white masses and get away from crosshatching and shading for middletone effects. I make extensive use of shading film and Benday. On the Sunday Magazine, which carries colors, I try to stick to solids as much as I can. That's all I can say about the work of myself, except that being Mexican of father and mother, makes me one of about two or three working on American newspapers. That's all,

                              Yours obediently,

                              Alex

11

ACTUAL SIZE OF
THE ORIGINAL DRAWING

Work out one figure at a time and do many of them, then it will be easy for you to put two or three figures in a drawing. It is so easy to start drawings that are far beyond your experience and in so doing many become discouraged and quit. The ones that are stickers will hit their stride and fall into the line of art work for which they are best fitted.

One of the most frequent questions asked is, "how and where do you get your ideas." Do not let this worry you too much, because you are given a story to read or are told what part to illustrate and what space it is to take in the paper, magazine, etc.

Pay special attention to the three pages in front of this book, on how to layout a drawing with T square and triangle. This will save you many a mistake and time in trying to figure out your reductions. It is SO simple, once you understand.

MOST COMIC STRIP ARTISTS ARE VERY SERIOUS AND CONSERVATIVE. THEY MUST BE THINKERS, ABLE TO GRASP THE OTHER PERSON'S POINT OF VIEW. THEY ARE SALESMEN, SELLING THE PUBLIC LAUGHS, AND TO BE SUCCESSFUL MUST UNDERSTAND PSYCHOLOGY AND APPLY IT TO EVERY DRAWING THEY MAKE.

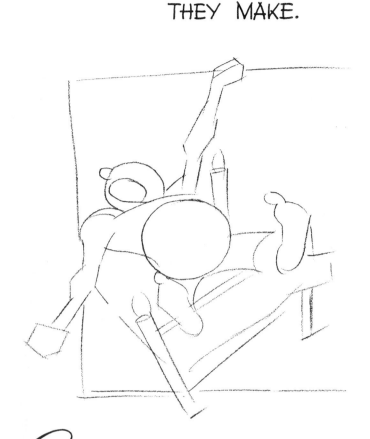 

CARTOONISTS MUST DEVELOP SOMETHING **UNUSUAL**, SOMETHING DIFFERENT, TO RECEIVE THE PAY THEY DO. I HAVE USED THE WORD "DEVELOP", WEBSTER COLLEGIATE SAYS, "DEVELOP" MEANS "TO UNFOLD BY DEGREES, REVEAL, DISCOVER". THIS PART OF COMICS SO FEW STUDENTS UNDERSTAND.

DO NOT LET SOME HIGH PRESSURE SALESLETTER OR SALESMAN MAKE YOU BELIEVE THAT UNDER THEIR GUIDANCE YOU WILL BE A WORLDBEATER WITHIN THREE MONTHS, UNLESS YOU WISH TO PAY OUT YOUR GOOD MONEY FOR FLATTERY.

ALWAYS MARK YOUR MEASUREMENTS LIKE THIS ON YOUR DRAWING FOR THE REDUCTION

|←——————— 8" ———————→|

Artists I know are all firm believers in the use of the eraser. This, of course, does not mean that scribbling or a great number of lines will help you. The better ground-work you have in your drawing, the less effort it will be for you to put your ideas on paper.

Here let me correct the mistaken idea that so many beginners have, that artists, after they have been in the business a number of years, have no need to block in their drawings, but start to ink in, eliminating all pencil work. I know many of the topnotchers and cannot recall one that would even think of inking in a drawing without first blocking in with pencil.

15

*Y*our pencil drawings are the most essential, see that they are clean cut, not messy — erase all unnecessary lines before inking in with brush or pen. Use a blue pencil if you wish, then you do not have to erase your lines, as blue will not photograph. Of course your drawing looks much better clean of all pencil lines.

ON'T feel that you have to copy anything line for line, drawing it as you see it, using the step drawings to help get it started right. In this way you will work into a style all your own. Try also to draw the heads facing a different way. Use a pocket mirror, holding it alongside of the drawing. This will help you change the drawing you are working from face the opposite way. Try, and keep on trying — that is the way one learns.

*T*ry to visualize how you would feel if this happened to you and put that feeling into it. Yes, put yourself in the little animals' place also and imagine their reaction and you have the elements for a good cartoon.

Surely, work from clippings. Eventually you will have sufficient experience to draw from memory.

Your ideas may be obtained through radio, by reading, traveling or association with people who think. New ideas are not confined to working hours. I have planned my work in many different places, on subways in New York City to movie lots in Hollywood and from Mexico to Alaska on trains, planes and boats. Jot down thoughts as they come to you. They may be worth gold—and again they may not be worth the paper they are written upon; only time and the way you develop them can answer that. I hope "there's gold in them thar hills" for you.

Yours for success,
W. T. F.

Try these little figures that Alex has created. I will give you a start by showing how you can block them in. One of the big secrets of this type of art work is the brush strokes and this will come only by diligent practice of hundreds of brush strokes, so that you will eventually know beforehand, just what sort of stroke you will make.

Smart little figures like these are a fine asset to your work.

The little girl that Hal has developed has lots of possibilities and you will see her and her little pooch in your favorite comic section one of these days. Mr. Rasmusson is coming to pay me a visit soon and I am looking forward to showing him Southern California and the Radio and Movie Studios.

By courtesy of Geo Stanley

HAL. RASMUSSON

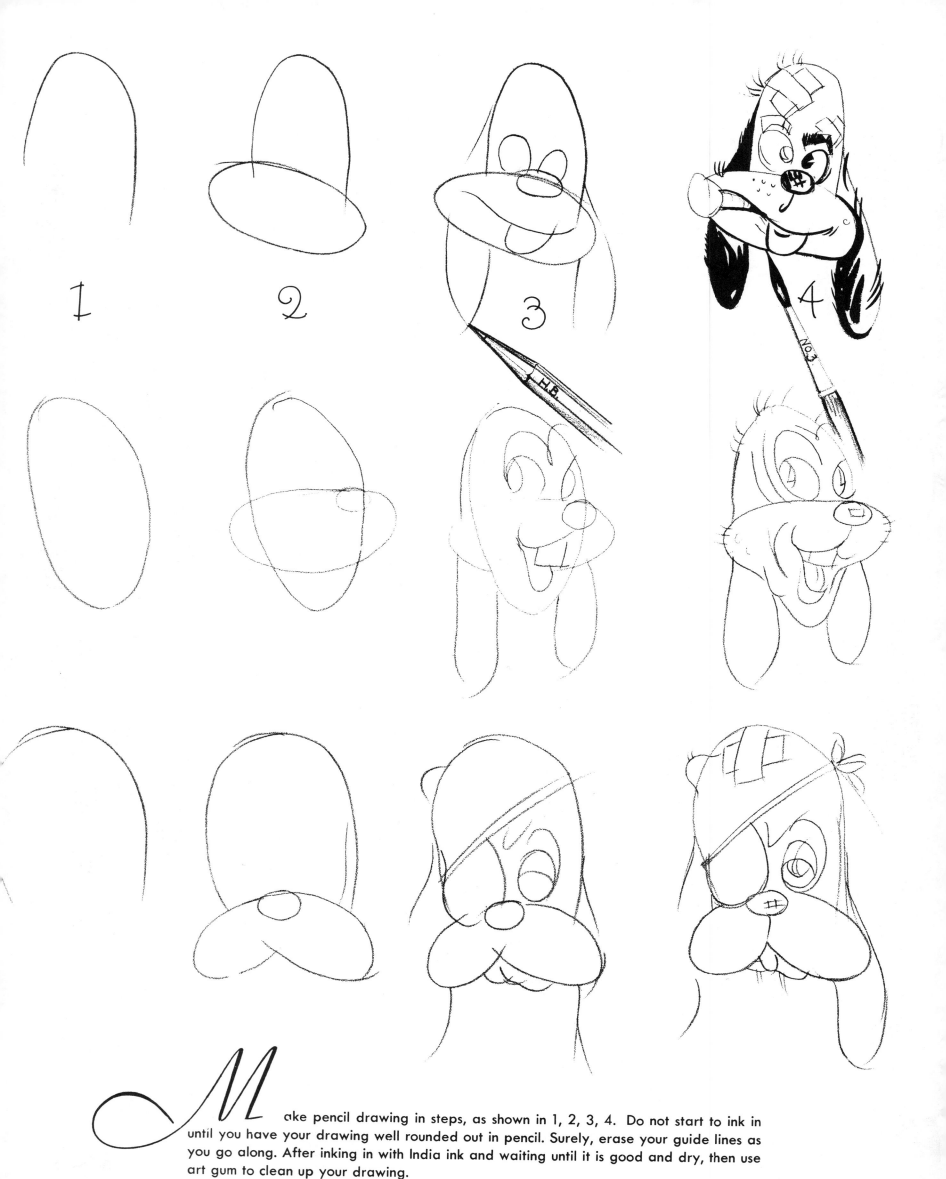

*M*ake pencil drawing in steps, as shown in 1, 2, 3, 4. Do not start to ink in until you have your drawing well rounded out in pencil. Surely, erase your guide lines as you go along. After inking in with India ink and waiting until it is good and dry, then use art gum to clean up your drawing.

Hal.Rasmusson 25

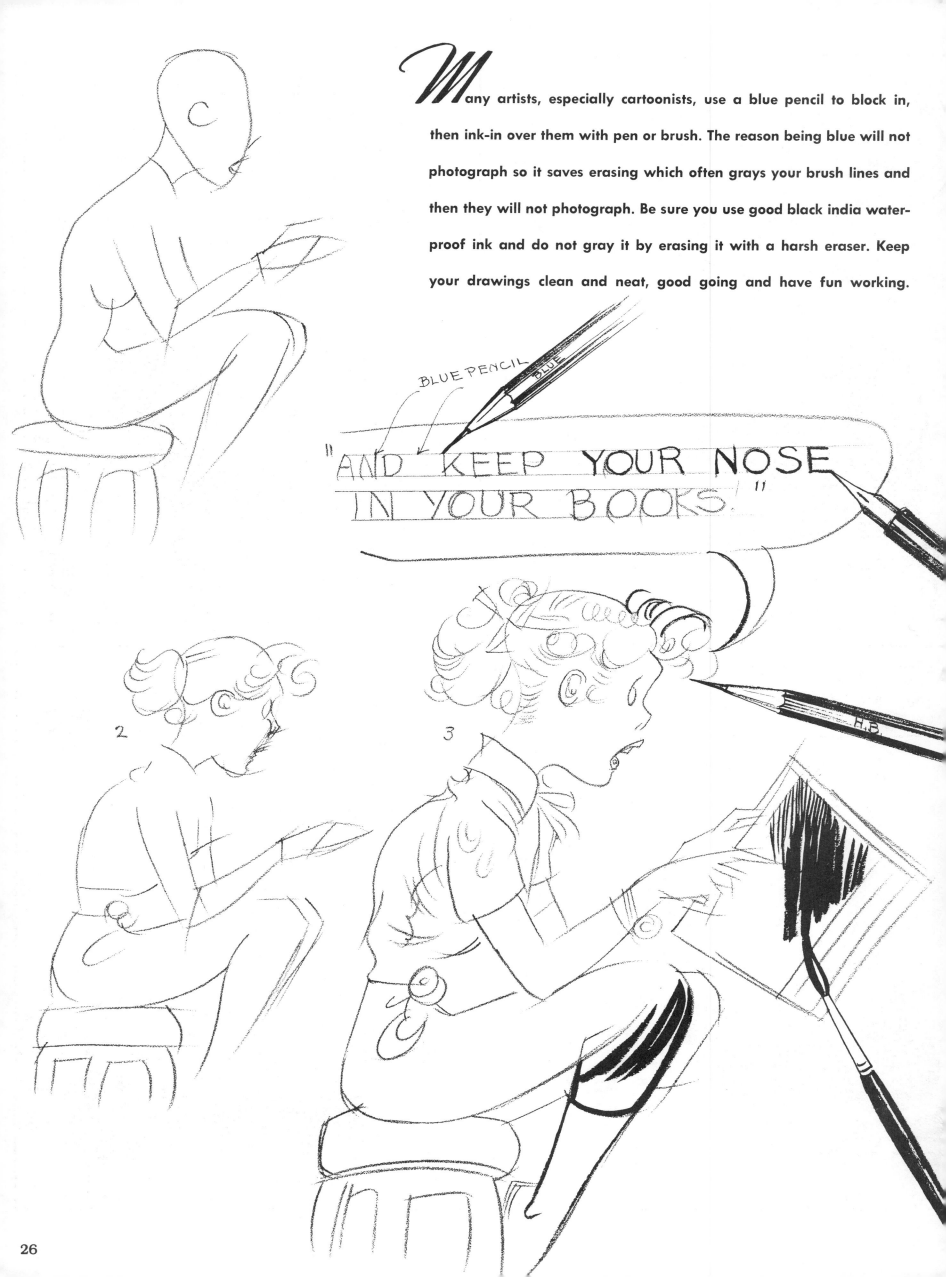

Many artists, especially cartoonists, use a blue pencil to block in, then ink-in over them with pen or brush. The reason being blue will not photograph so it saves erasing which often grays your brush lines and then they will not photograph. Be sure you use good black india waterproof ink and do not gray it by erasing it with a harsh eraser. Keep your drawings clean and neat, good going and have fun working.

BLUE PENCIL

BLUE

"AND KEEP YOUR NOSE IN YOUR BOOKS!"

2

3

A small watercolor box and a good #8 brush will be enough to give
you fine practice coloring in your drawings like Mr. Rasmusson. Remember,
make a nice drawing in pencil then ink it in with India waterproof ink, let
dry, then use your watercolor. Start with light yellow, add red for cheeks
while moist. Surely thin with water. Shall we try? Fine!

Hal Rasmusson and all cartoonists work ahead from 6 weeks to 6 months so as not to be late, due to vacation, sickness, etc. This is the same size as original, then it is reduced to about one-half this size when you see it in the paper.

Materials You Will Need

RULING PEN
OR
RIGHT LINE PEN

FILL RULING PEN FOUNTAIN WITH BRUSH OR QUILL THAT COMES ON THE CORK OF INDIA INK

H.B. PENCIL
THUMB TACKS
ERASERS — RED RUBBER AND ART GUM TO CLEAN YOUR DRAWING WITH.
BRUSHES — NO. 1 AND NO. 3 GOOD SABLE WATER COLOR BRUSHES.
PENS AND HOLDERS — 170-290 POINTS, SMALL LETTERING PENS IF YOU WANT AND OF COURSE LOTS OF PRACTICE PAPER.
2-PLY BRISTOL BOARD — HOT AND COLD PRESSED, FOR FINISHED WORK.

ART GUM

ABC

AS YOU GO ALONG, YOU CAN ADD DIFFERENT PAPERS AND CRAYONS. DO NOT LET THIS SCARE YOU.

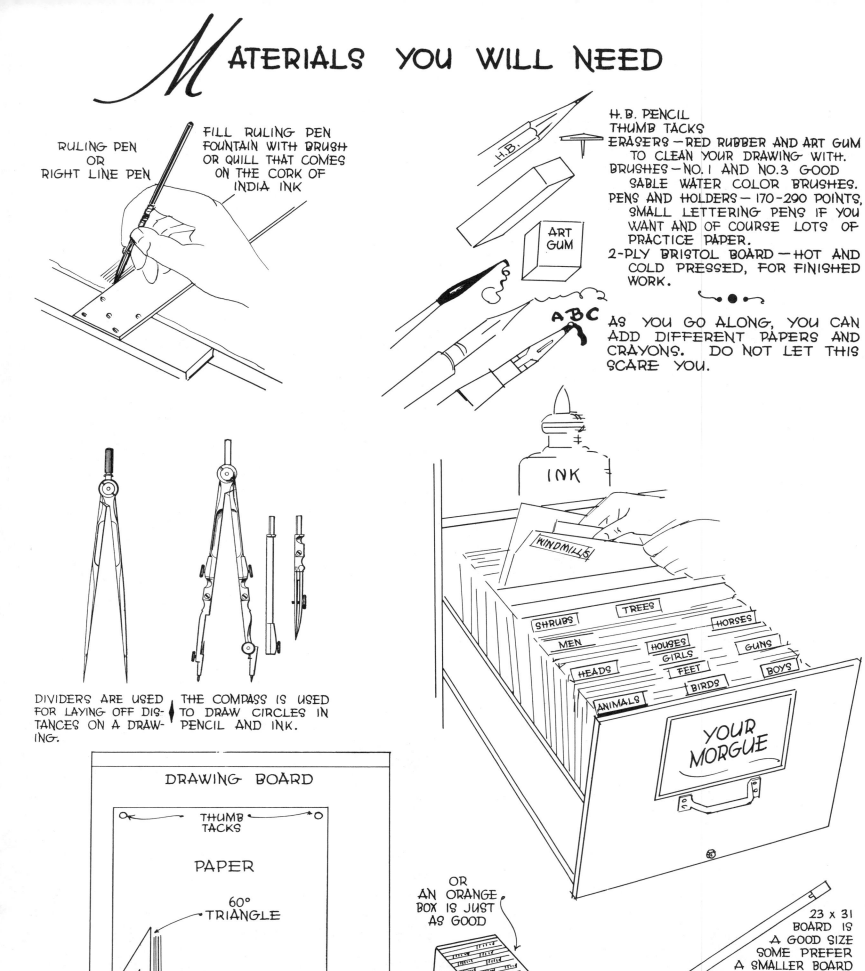

INK

WINDMILLS

SHRUBS   TREES   HORSES
MEN   HOUSES   GUNS
GIRLS
HEADS   FEET   BOYS
BIRDS
ANIMALS

YOUR MORGUE

DIVIDERS ARE USED FOR LAYING OFF DISTANCES ON A DRAWING.

THE COMPASS IS USED TO DRAW CIRCLES IN PENCIL AND INK.

DRAWING BOARD

THUMB TACKS

PAPER

60° TRIANGLE

T SQUARE

OR AN ORANGE BOX IS JUST AS GOOD

23 x 31 BOARD IS A GOOD SIZE SOME PREFER A SMALLER BOARD

REST BOARD ON TABLE AND HOLD ON LAP AT ABOUT THIS SLANT

WHEN SENDING DRAWINGS TO PUBLISHERS, ALWAYS MAIL FLAT. (A 9 x 12 ENVELOPE IS BEST FOR A START). DO NOT FORGET TO PRINT YOUR NAME AND ADDRESS ON BACK OF EACH DRAWING AND ENCLOSE POSTAGE FOR THEIR RETURN.

YOUR STUDIO

THIS IS VERY ESSENTIAL, IT NEED NOT BE FANCY, JUST A CORNER IN THE GARAGE, BASEMENT OR YOUR ROOM. SEE THAT YOUR DRAWING BOARD IS PLACED WHERE THE LIGHT COMES IN OVER YOUR LEFT SHOULDER, (IF YOU ARE LEFT HANDED, OVER YOUR RIGHT SHOULDER.) YES, ARRANGE LIGHT FROM SAME DIRECTION FOR NIGHT WORK.

MANY OF OUR BEST ARTISTS ARE LEFT HANDED. DO NOT LET ANY ONE TALK YOU OUT OF IT.

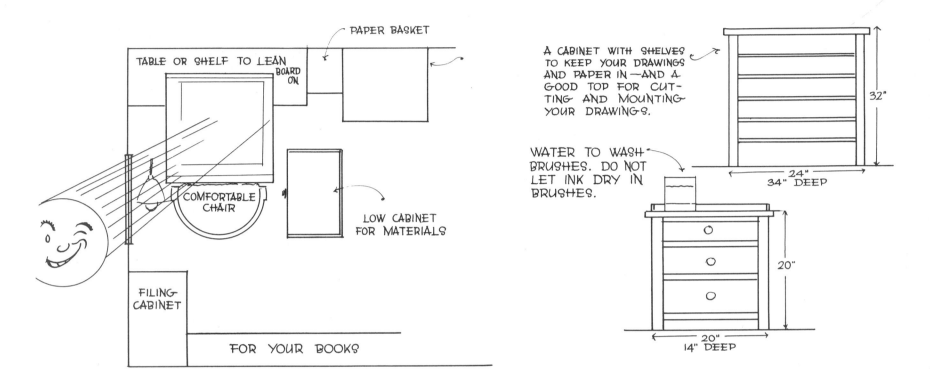

PAPER BASKET

TABLE OR SHELF TO LEAN BOARD ON

COMFORTABLE CHAIR

LOW CABINET FOR MATERIALS

FILING CABINET

FOR YOUR BOOKS

A CABINET WITH SHELVES TO KEEP YOUR DRAWINGS AND PAPER IN —AND A GOOD TOP FOR CUTTING AND MOUNTING YOUR DRAWINGS.

32"

24"
34" DEEP

WATER TO WASH BRUSHES. DO NOT LET INK DRY IN BRUSHES.

20"

20"
14" DEEP

A note to Mother, Wifie, Dad or Sis:—

Please do not fuss at our pal here, because he or she does not put away their drawing materials after each time they work. They should have a den or corner they can call their own, with a "no trespassing" understanding with it, and for heaven's sake never clean up or destroy what you may consider junk; it might be a prized possession.

Now a note to you, my sprouting artist.

If the folks assign a spot to you, see that it is kept orderly and clean, even with your materials out ready for work, and this is necessary because, if you have to get ready each time, chances are you will put it off and not work at all. Lay out your work so you can sit down and start right in.

My first corner was in our basement, next to the furnace, warm in winter, cool in summer and no one to bother. There the small foundation was laid that became my life's work. "Art is long" they say but may I add worth every moment of it.

Good luck and success, As Ever.

Walter T. Foster

More Ways To Learn...With Walter Foster!

BEGINNERS ART SERIES
Introductory Art Skills

Looking for a way to spend "quality time" with the children in your life? Introduce them to the wonderful world of art...with the **Beginners Art Series** by Walter Foster Publishing. For $5.95 per title, this innovative instructional series teaches them the basics of art and art theory...expands their creativity...and develops their tactile and visual skills. Children ages six and up will be enthralled for hours...whether it's *Drawing Fun, Color*

Fun, Clay Fun, Comic Strip Fun, Poster/ Lettering Fun, Paper Art Fun...or all six titles. Written by experts in art education, these books provide demonstrations with easy-to-understand instructions and follow a standardized format including: a glossary of art vocabulary, a section on materials listing the tools associated with each topic, and a series of exciting projects for "hands on" creative experience.

HOW TO SERIES
Developing Art Skills

Now you can develop your art skills...easily and economically! The **How To Series** shows you how with art books addressing all media—pencil, watercolor, oil, acrylic, pen & ink, charcoal and pastel...and a variety of subject matter—animals, cartoons, figures, landscapes, seascapes, still life and more.
Written by accomplished artists, the books in the **How To Series** will help you improve your skills to become the best

artist you can be! You will enjoy exploring the basics of form, line and dimension ...and learn the intricacies of advanced rendering techniques. You'll learn secrets that have helped our authors achieve excellence in their artistic specialties. There are over 100 titles in the Walter Foster **How To Series.** At only $3.95 per title these books fit every budget!

ARTIST'S LIBRARY SERIES
Advanced Art Skills

If you're serious about art, you don't want to be without the books in the Walter Foster **Artist's Library Series.** Focusing on a specific medium, subject or technique, each of these books teaches you complete procedures, from beginning to end.
The **Artist's Library Series** offers books addressing oil painting, watercolors, pencil drawing, acrylics, color theory, pen & ink, colored pencils, pastels, airbrush,

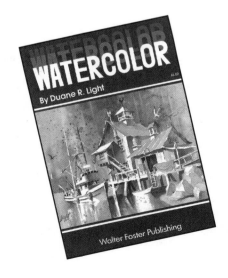

calligraphy, impressionism, dry-brush watercolor, perspective and cartooning. You will find that these books are invaluable reference guides...No other texts offer such unique instruction at such a reasonable price—only $5.95 per title. The **Artist's Library Series** is sure to be a welcome addition to your library of art books!

Walter Foster Publishing ...The most recognized name in art publishing for more than 73 years.